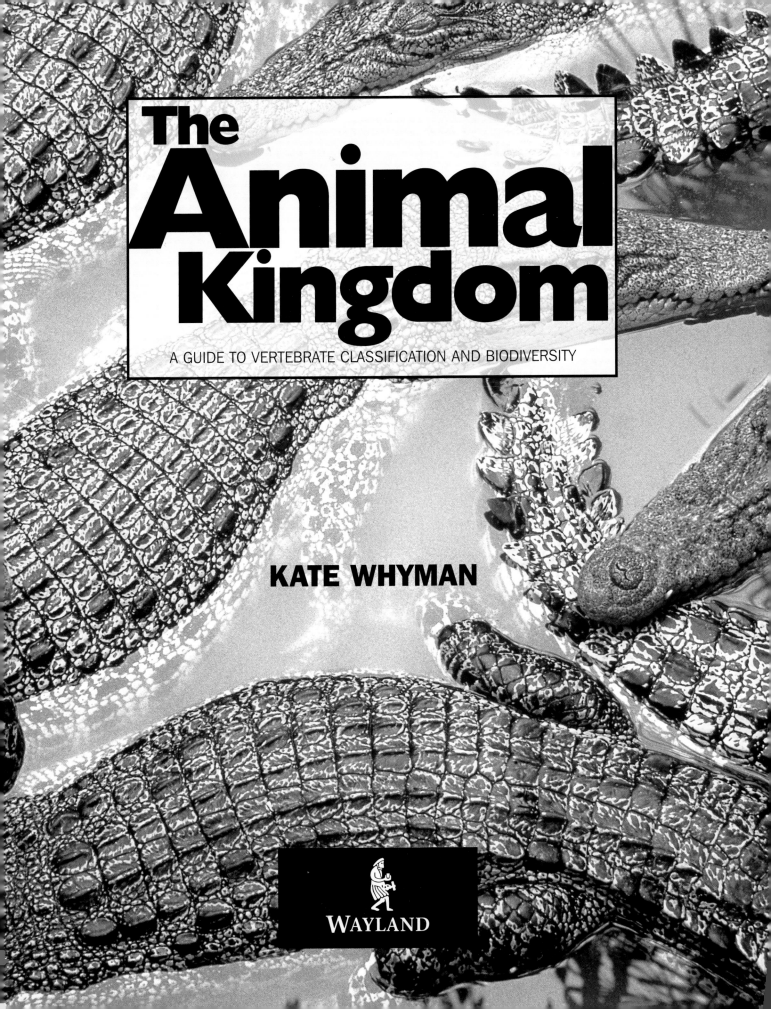

The Animal Kingdom

A GUIDE TO VERTEBRATE CLASSIFICATION AND BIODIVERSITY

KATE WHYMAN

WAYLAND

First published in 1999 by Wayland Publishers Limited
61 Western Road, Hove, East Sussex BN3 1JD, England

British Library Cataloguing in Publication Data
Whyman, Kathryn
  The Animal Kingdom : a guide to the classification and
biodiversity of vertebrates. - (Classification)
  1. Vertebrates   2. Vertebrates - Classification
  3. Zoology - Environmental aspects
  I. Title
  596
ISBN 0 7502 2455 X

Consultant: Carol Levick, Education Unit,
  Natural History Museum
Editor: Margot Richardson
Designer: Simon Borrough

Printed and bound in Italy by G. Canale & C. S. p. A.

Cover captions: main picture: *Toucan in Costa Rica*. Small pictures, from left: *Leopard; Green Iguana; Eastern Screech Owl; Spinecheek Clownfish; Blue Poison Arrow Frog.*

Title page: *An overhead view of crocodiles, crowded together in a pool.*

Below: *Blue tits feed their young on caterpillars. Feeding is busiest in the mornings when the adult may make up to 72 trips to the nest each hour!*

Find Wayland on the Internet at http://www.wayland.co.uk

Contents

Kingdoms of life

THERE ARE WELL OVER TWO MILLION types of living organisms on earth, and more are being discovered all the time. All of these organisms have certain characteristics in common: they all grow and reproduce, they all take in substances they need and get rid of substances they do not, and they all respire, move, and respond to their environments. But in spite of these similarities, there is an amazing variety among living things, from simple single-celled organisms to mammals as highly developed as dolphins and humans.

There are two species of elephant. This is the African elephant, Loxodonta africana. *It is the largest land animal in the world. The other species is the Indian elephant,* Elephas maximus.

Classifying living things

Putting living things into groups and giving them names makes it easier to talk about them and understand them. This process of sorting is called classification. Most scientists classify all living things into one of five large groups, called kingdoms: Animals, Plants, Fungi, Protists (which include algae) and Monerans (which include bacteria and blue-green algae). Kingdoms are made up of organisms that share some basic similarities but are also very different. For example, the animal kingdom contains animals as diverse as an earthworm and an eagle.

However, each kingdom can be divided into smaller and smaller groups, each containing organisms that have more and more features in common. The smallest group, a species, describes any group of living things that have two major characteristics: first, they all share the same general physical appearance; second, and more importantly, members of a species can successfully reproduce.

The science of classifying living things is called taxonomy, and someone who classifies living things is known as a taxonomist. Taxonomists try to group living things together which seem to be related. To do this, they look for physical features, such as whether or not an animal has hair or scales, as well as chemical and genetic similarities. Sometimes it is clear how to classify a particular species, but sometimes it is not, and taxonomists may disagree.

The system of classification used today is based on the work of the eighteenth-century Swedish botanist, Carolus Linnaeus. Linnaeus also developed a way of naming living things using Latin.

Most animals have common names, such as 'spider' or 'frog'. But there are thousands of species of frog, and even more of spiders. What's more, these common names vary in different languages and countries. In the Linnaeus system, however, each species has one Latin name which is the same the world over. The first word in the name represents the genus the organism belongs to, and begins with a capital letter. The second is its particular species name.

This book looks at similarities and differences between a group of animals that all have backbones – the vertebrates. Vertebrates include five classes of animals: fish, amphibians, reptiles, birds, mammals.

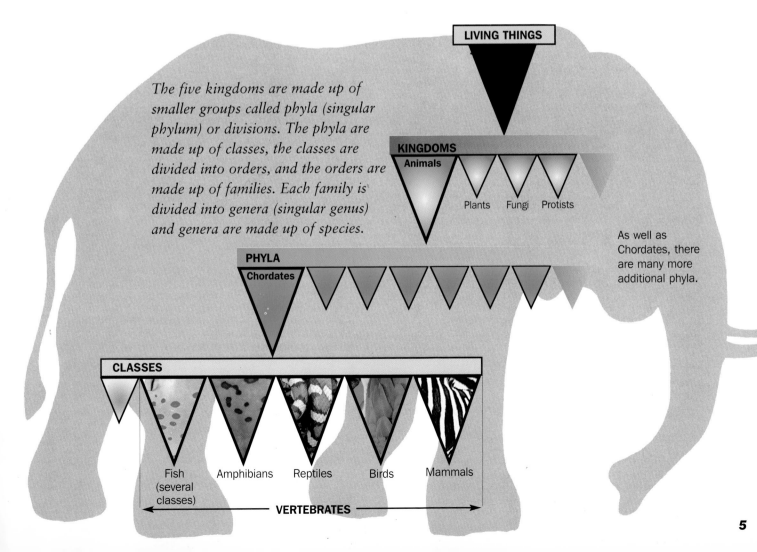

The five kingdoms are made up of smaller groups called phyla (singular phylum) or divisions. The phyla are made up of classes, the classes are divided into orders, and the orders are made up of families. Each family is divided into genera (singular genus) and genera are made up of species.

LIVING THINGS

KINGDOMS
Animals
Plants Fungi Protists

As well as Chordates, there are many more additional phyla.

PHYLA
Chordates

CLASSES
Fish (several classes) Amphibians Reptiles Birds Mammals
VERTEBRATES

Fish

FISH BEGAN TO APPEAR in the oceans more than 400 million years ago. There are now some 30,000 species and they have adapted to live in almost every water habitat on earth. Fish are superbly adapted for living in water. Their streamlined bodies allow them to move through the water with ease, and their gills enable them to extract oxygen from the water.

▲ *The world's largest fish is the whale shark* (Rhincodon typus) *which can be 15 m or more long.*

Characteristics of fish:
- ▶ breathe with gills
- ▶ have scaly skin
- ▶ live in water
- ▶ have fins and muscular tails for swimming.

Almost three-quarters of the earth's surface is covered by water, from ponds and streams to rivers, lakes and oceans. Fish are found in nearly every body of water apart from the very salty water of the Dead Sea and some hot springs. Most species of fish live in the oceans, with only about 2,500 species living in fresh water.

Fish can be divided into two main groups. By far the biggest group (about 24,000 species) is the bony fish. As their name suggests, these fish have skeletons made of bone. Goldfish, cod and tuna are all types of bony fish.

The other group has skeletons made of cartilage. Cartilaginous fish include sharks, skates, rays and chimaeras, which are very efficient hunters. Another group of cartilaginous fish is the jawless fish. There are only 85 species of jawless fish.

Fish bodies

Many fish are extremely well streamlined, with sharp pointed heads and very smooth bodies. This is particularly important for animals that move through water, as water is 800 times as dense as air: any part of the body that juts out will slow the fish down quite considerably.

Most bony fish have a swim bladder. This is a gas-filled bag that holds the fish up in the water. By adjusting the amount of gas in its swim bladder, the fish can control its position: the more gas in the swim bladder, the higher the fish floats in the water. Bony fish use their fins to fine tune their steering.

Sharks and rays are more dense than water. In order to prevent themselves from sinking they have to keep swimming. A shark's powerful tail propels it forward, and it uses its fins to steer itself upwards.

This blue spotted stingray (Taeniura lymma) *spends most of its time on the ocean floor, so its body shape does not need to be as streamlined as other fish, which swim much more.*

Salt and fresh water

One of the problems for marine fish is that the ocean has a greater concentration of salts than the fishes' own body fluids. This means that marine fish tend to lose water to the sea by a process called osmosis. To make up for this loss, these fish constantly drink sea water and excrete salt.

Freshwater fish have the opposite problem: water tends to enter their bodies from their environment. To compensate, they have large kidneys and excrete lots of urine. They also drink very little.

Species such as the salmon, which travel between sea water and fresh water, have to spend a short period in brackish water to allow their bodies to adapt to the new conditions.

Being aware of the environment

Most fish have well-developed senses. While sharks and rays can see only in black and white, bony fish can see colours clearly. Many bony fish are brightly patterned, especially those that live in clear, sunlit water where their colours are visible. Fish also have good hearing and are aware of all the noises that other water-living animals make, such as shells clicking and tails slapping in the water.

Certain fish have ways of 'seeing' in the dark. The South American electric eel lives in tropical rivers that are so covered with floating vegetation that they are completely black. The eel has special muscles that generate an electric charge. Any object in the water disrupts the pattern of charge and the eel becomes aware of the difference through receptor pores spaced out over its body.

Some species have organs that produce an electrical field, which can be used to stun prey, inform the fish of changes in its environment, and for communication.

▲ *This catfish* (Synodontis multipunctatus) *has well-developed whisker-like structures called barbels around its mouth that help it to feel its way. In many species, the barbels are covered with taste buds that also give the fish a good sense of taste.*

All fish have one sense that other animals do not have. Down the sides of their bodies runs a line of pores, connected by a canal just below the surface. This is the lateral line. It enables fish to detect differences of pressure in the water so that they are aware of currents and depth. They can also sense the movements of other fish swimming alongside them, which is particularly important for those that swim in shoals.

Some fish can see above the water and below it at the same time. The archer fish (Toxotes chatereus) eats insects and spiders that may settle on plants growing on river banks. It takes aim and squirts a jet of drops, knocking the insect into the water so it can be eaten

(1) *The male stickleback defends his territory from other males.*

(2) *He starts to build a nest.*

Breeding

Most bony fish lay eggs (which are also called spawn), sometimes in vast numbers. For example, cod typically produce between four and eight million eggs per year. These are laid in the open sea, and probably no more than 10 per cent of them will survive to become adults. Those species that produce small numbers of eggs usually protect them in nests, or even in their mouths. Some cartilaginous fish also lay eggs, but others bear live young.

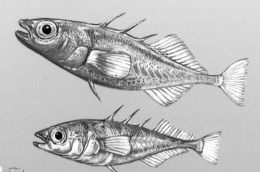

(3) *When the nest is ready he begins to court a female stckleback who is ready to lay eggs.*

(4) *He shows her the nest.*

Courtship and mating

Elaborate courting rituals are found in some fish. This page shows the stages in the courtship of the stickleback. In the mating season, the male stickleback develops a red belly and bright blue eyes. First he establishes his territory and prepares a nest. Next, he attracts a female by performing a dance and showing her his nest. Once in the nest, the female lays her eggs, which the male later fertilizes. It is the job of the male to tend the nest. He wafts water over the eggs, which ensures they have enough oxygen, When they hatch into small fry he guards them from predators.

(5) *The female enters the nest and lays her eggs.*

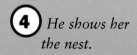

(6) *The male then fertilizes the eggs.*

(7) *The male looks after the fry when they hatch.*

10

Salmon may have to overcome great obstacles to return to their breeding grounds, even leaping up waterfalls. This brown bear (Ursus arctos) is hunting the migrating fish.

Migrating fish

Some fish, such as eels and salmon, travel long distances to find the best places to lay their eggs.

Salmon spend part of their lives in rivers and part in the sea. Female salmon lay their eggs on riverbeds. The eggs hatch and the young salmon stay in the river until they are two or three years old. They then start their journey to the sea. On the way they may face many hazards, such as being eaten by birds and other fish. They may also have to cope with wide temperature differences between the river and the sea, and the move to a saltier environment. If they survive the journey, the salmon stay at sea for about four years, returning to the river when they are ready to lay eggs.

The journey back to the river may be hundreds or even thousands of kilometres long. But salmon have powerful, streamlined bodies which help them swim more easily upstream through fast currents. When the river levels are high they can travel as many as 30 km per day.

Amphibians

AMPHIBIANS EVOLVED FROM FISH about 350 million years ago. They were the first vertebrates to colonize the land.

The name amphibian comes from Greek and means 'living a double life'. This refers to the fact that many amphibians have two distinct stages of life: the young larva, or tadpole, which lives in water, and the adult which lives on land. The process by which the tadpole develops into the adult is called metamorphosis.

Characteristics of amphibians:
► have smooth, moist skin
► live in damp places
► breathe through their skins as well as with lungs.

Caecilians may look like earthworms but in fact, like other amphibians, they have backbones. This is the South American Cecilia tentaculata.

Today there are three surviving groups of amphibians: the frogs and toads, the newts and salamanders, and the caecilians, also known as blind worms. There are about 4,500 amphibian species altogether, 4,000 of which are frogs and toads. Though frogs tend to have somewhat smoother skins than toads, there are no clear ways of distinguishing between the two of them.

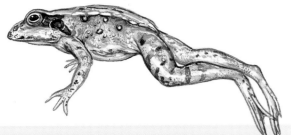

Although the majority of species live in the tropics, there are amphibians living all over the world, except in places where there is not enough water. Like fish and reptiles, their body temperature changes with the temperature of their environment, and in cold climates they hibernate in order to survive the winter.

Living on the land poses quite different problems from living in water, and adult amphibians have developed different ways of moving and breathing from their tadpole forms. While tadpoles swim using fins and powerful tails, most adult amphibians have four limbs strong enough to support the weight of the body, which enable them to walk and jump. However, the caecilians are legless and move by burrowing underground.

While tadpoles use gills to breathe in water, these are no use for breathing in air so adult amphibians have developed lungs. However, most have lungs that are too small to provide enough oxygen and amphibians breathe through their skins as well. Skin can only be used for breathing if it is soft and is kept damp. For this reason, amphibians can never stray too far from water. If they do, they are in danger of drying up and dying.

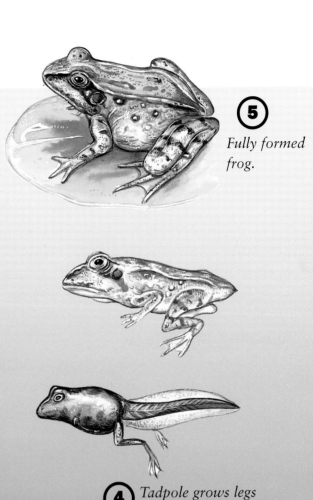

(5) *Fully formed frog.*

(4) *Tadpole grows legs and loses its tail.*

(3) *Tadpole loses gills and grows lungs to breathe air.*

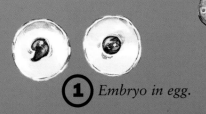

(1) *Embryo in egg.*

gills

(2) *Egg hatches as a tadpole with gills to breathe.*

Life cycle of a frog
A frog's egg hatches out as a tadpole, with gills for breathing and a tail for swimming. Gradually it grows legs, loses its tail and gills, and develops lungs for breathing in air. It is now an adult and ready to live on land.

Breeding

Most amphibians lay eggs. But unlike the eggs of a bird, these eggs have no protective, waterproof shell. Instead they are covered in a jelly-like substance which can easily dry out in air. For this reason, most amphibians lay their eggs in water. Even here the eggs are far from safe. Many are eaten by insect larvae and flatworms. And even those that hatch into tadpoles are then pounced on by water beetles, dragonfly larvae and fish. The loss is enormous, but then so is the number of eggs laid. A female toad may lay as many as 20,000 eggs each season.

Avoiding predators

Amphibians have various ways of protecting themselves from predators. Most hide during the day and are active only at night. A frog's leap is more than just a way of getting around, it is also a very effective way of escaping from an enemy. Some are very well camouflaged, matching the colours of the leaves they rest among. Others have bright colouration and alarming displays that warn off predators.

Feeding

Many amphibians, especially frogs and toads, have developed a very effective way of catching prey. Not particularly fast-moving animals, they have instead a long, sticky tongue which can be flicked out very quickly to catch insects. Amphibians cannot chew, but the tongue helps the prey pass through the mouth – and so do the eyes! When a frog swallows it blinks at the same time. Its eyes bulge into the roof of the mouth and help to push food to the back of the throat.

Senses

Most amphibians have a well-developed sense of touch, but their other senses vary a great deal. Those that live underground or in caves have little need for sight, while those that live in trees or in clear water can see well. Frogs and toads, which have remarkably loud voices, also have eardrums. But other amphibians, that do not make sounds, do not seem to have a sense of hearing either.

Changing forms

A very few amphibians never grow up; instead they remain in their tadpole form all through their lives, even breeding in this form. The best known is the axolotl. Some salamanders have the option of remaining in tadpole form if there is enough water. Only when water is in short supply do they metamorphose into the adult form.

◀ *When under attack, this fire-bellied toad* (Bombina orientalis) *will throw itself on its back to display its red and black belly. Many amphibians secrete a slimy mucus that tastes unpleasant but this toad produces a bitter poison.*

▲ *This unusual amphibian* (Ambystoma mexicanum) *is an axolotl, meaning 'water monster'. It stays in tadpole form all its life, developing great branching gills on either side of its neck.*

Reptiles

REPTILES EVOLVED FROM AMPHIBIANS about 300 million years ago. There are about 6,500 species alive today, most of which live on land. Unlike amphibians, they have a waterproof skin that protects them from drying out, and they lay eggs with protective shells.

A type of lizard, this gecko (Gecko gecko) can walk on walls and upside-down on ceilings, thanks to the thousands of microscopic hairs under its toes that cling to even the slightest rough spot.

Characteristics of reptiles:
▶ have dry, waterproof skin with scales
▶ breathe with lungs
▶ have internal fertilization
▶ lay eggs with yolk and shells
▶ fully formed young emerge from the eggs.

A colourful mountain king snake (Lampropeltis pyromelana) *from Arizona, USA. In spite of its alarming colours, this snake is not poisonous.*

Like amphibians, a reptile's body temperature changes with the temperature of its environment. For this reason, most reptiles cannot survive in cold climates. However, they live in almost every warm environment, from the sea to swamps and rivers, rain forests and deserts. There are four orders of reptiles alive today: the snakes and lizards, the crocodilians, the tortoises and turtles, and the tuatara.

Reptiles manage to regulate their body temperatures quite effectively. Having a waterproof skin allows them to warm their blood by basking in the sun, without danger of drying up. As soon as their blood starts to become too hot they quickly head for the shade, or even for water, until their bodies are cool again.

Many reptiles can raise their bodies off the ground, which allows air to cool them. Crocodiles often rest with their mouths wide open. This allows heat to escape – and it also enables scavenging birds to pick their teeth. In fact, most reptiles manage to keep their body temperatures at about 37 °C, which is the normal body temperature of mammals. As reptiles use far less energy than a mammal for this, they have been able to colonize areas, such as deserts, where food is scarce.

Early reptiles

We think that dinosaurs first appeared about 210 million years ago and dominated the earth until they disappeared approximately 65 million years ago. Nobody knows quite why the dinosaurs died out, although many theories exist, but perhaps a change in climate was partly the cause.

Snakes

Snakes seem to have developed originally as burrowers. Their streamlined form and lack of legs would have helped them move easily through the ground. Snakes also have no ears that stick out – another advantage for life underground.

Today, most snakes live above ground, but they still have no legs. Instead, they move by sliding from side to side, but some can also creep up on prey by contracting along their length without moving sideways at all.

Some snakes kill by tightly squeezing their prey and suffocating them. These are the constrictors. Other snakes kill by poisoning. They may have fangs at the back of their mouths – which means they have to grip their prey for some time until the fangs have penetrated – or at the front.

Rattlesnakes have a special sense organ between each eye and a nostril called a pit. The pit is very sensitive to infrared radiation, or heat, and can detect a rise of just 0.03 of one degree. This means that the rattlesnake can track down prey very easily.

The rattlesnake also produces eggs with very thin shells, which enables the embryo to absorb nutrients from its mother's blood – quite like a mammalian placenta.

Cobras and mambas have fangs fixed to the front of the mouth.

▲ *The vipers and adders have long fangs that are hinged at the front of the mouth. When not in use, the fangs are folded back against the roof of the mouth. As soon as the snake opens its mouth to bite, the fangs swing downwards and forwards.*

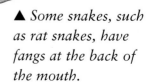

▲ *Some snakes, such as rat snakes, have fangs at the back of the mouth.*

Lizards

There are over 3,000 species of lizard worldwide. They include geckos, chameleons, monitors and iguanas. Although lizards belong to the same order as snakes, they are usually easy to tell apart. Most lizards have four legs, eyelids that move, eardrums and a fleshy tongue. However, some lizards are legless and look quite snake-like. These lizards usually burrow or live in habitats such as narrow crevices where having legs would be no advantage.

Lizards have various ways of defending themselves against enemies. Many can shed their tails – to distract a predator while they escape – and regrow them later. Some, like the chameleon, are very well camouflaged against their surroundings. Others put on alarming displays.

Tuatara

The tuatara is the only species of its order that has survived. It is the only reptile which does not have a penis, and it is different from lizards in that it is active at low temperatures, even below 7 °C.

It is found solely on small islands off New Zealand, where it shelters and lays its eggs in the nesting burrows of various sea-birds. The tuatara has hardly changed since the time of the dinosaurs, and the structure of its skull is similar to some reptile fossils. It grows up to 70 cm long, is greenish black, and has a spiny crest down its back.

Most chameleons live in trees. The long tail of this species from Madagascar (Parsonii cristifer) *can be used to help the animal grip on to branches.*

Crocodilians

The crocodilian order includes crocodiles, alligators and caimans. These have remained virtually unchanged for 200 million years and are the bulkiest of today's reptiles, with cigar-shaped bodies and short legs. They are found mainly near swamps, lakes and rivers, and are often seen floating in the water like logs, with only their nostrils, eyes, and ears above the surface. They can stay under water for long periods, and can even close their nostrils, but they must surface to breathe. Crocodilians have long, powerful tails that propel them when swimming. But they can also move surprisingly quickly on land.

The largest group is the crocodiles. Though crocodiles all live in or near water, they come ashore to lay eggs. In some species, the female lays over 100 hard-shelled eggs in holes or mounds of vegetation. She guards the eggs until they hatch and then carries the hatchlings down to the water in her mouth.

This alligator (Alligator mississipiensis) *lives in the southern states of the USA and grows to about 4 m in length. There are only two species of alligator; the other comes from China.*

Large numbers of female olive ridley turtles (Lepidochelys olivacea) *gather together on beaches to nest. Each turtle may lay between 100 and 110 eggs at a time, but only about 5 per cent of these eggs are able to hatch successfully.*

Young crocodiles eat worms and insects, but as they mature they add frogs and small fish to their diet. Adults are fierce hunters. They will attack animals the size of antelopes and even, occasionally, people. Some can live for up to a hundred years.

Tortoises and turtles

Tortoises and turtles are the only reptiles with bony shells as part of their skeletons. Many can pull their heads and legs inside their shells, making it difficult for predators to eat them. Some species pull their necks straight back into their shells. Others bend their necks sideways and curl their heads under the front of their upper shell.

The shells vary, from highly domed to nearly flat, depending on the sort of environment in which the animal lives and how it moves.

Legs also vary in shape. Land tortoises have column-shaped legs with claws. Pond turtles, which move on land as well as in water, have webbing between their claws. But sea turtles, which are excellent swimmers, have legs that have developed into oar-shaped flippers.

All tortoises and turtles lay eggs, usually in a hole in the sand or earth. Turtles often travel long distances to lay their eggs on the beaches where they themselves hatched out.

While young land tortoises eat worms and insects as well as plants, adults, which move too slowly to catch prey, eat flowers, fruits and plants. Sea turtles eat shellfish, jellyfish, fish and sea grasses, while freshwater turtles eat a range of animals including worms, frogs and fish.

Birds

BIRDS EVOLVED FROM REPTILES about 140 million years ago. There are about 9,000 species alive today, including parrots, penguins, humming-birds, kookaburras, owls and ostriches. Most birds can fly. They are adapted for flight by having wings instead of front legs, a light skeleton with hollow bones, and a covering of feathers.

Birds occupy every region of the planet. There are species that are able to survive the most extreme climates, from the frozen wastes of the Antarctic to the scorching heat of deserts, and even, in some cases, the great oceans. Some groups have lost the ability to fly and have become swift runners. Others are mainly swimmers. But most have perfected the art of flying.

Birds are extremely well-adapted for flying. Their feathers are slightly curved to form perfect aerofoils; as air passes over and under them the bird is lifted upwards. Being light in weight is an advantage for a flying animal. A bird the size of a swan may have as many as 25,000 feathers, but as feathers are made of keratin – the same substance as nails and hair, which is both light and strong – most large birds are still able to get off the ground.

Birds have thin bones and their long flying bones are hollow, often supported by cross-struts similar to those used in an aeroplane wing. Their lungs extend into air sacs that bulge into the body cavity and this also contributes to reducing their weight.

Characteristics of birds:

▶ the only animals with feathers
▶ breathe with lungs
▶ can control their body temperature internally
▶ have internal fertilization
▶ lay eggs with hard, waterproof shells
▶ usually incubate eggs with the heat of their bodies.

The African ostrich (Struthio camelus) *is the world's largest living bird. A male may be up to 2.7 m tall and weigh up to 156 kg. The ostrich cannot fly but it can run up to 70 kph when fleeing from danger.*

Wing shapes

The shape of a bird's wings affects how fast and far it can fly.

Albatross
The albatross has long slender wings for gliding in strong winds above the oceans.

Buzzard
The buzzard's broad wings enable it to soar while searching for prey.

Swallow
The swallow has curved, pointed wings and can fly fast, making sudden changes of direction as it hunts for insects.

Jay
The jay has rounded wings that it flaps slowly as it twists and turns through trees.

Sparrow
Most small birds, like the sparrow, have wings that allow them to fly quickly for short distances.

Humming-bird

A humming-bird's stiff, narrow wings beat 50 to 80 times a minute, producing a high pitched hum. Its wing action allows it to hover while feeding on nectar and it is the only bird that can fly backwards.

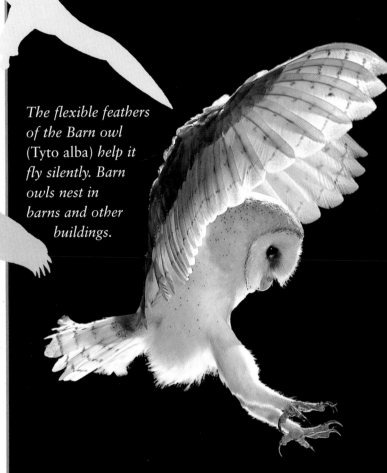

The flexible feathers of the Barn owl (Tyto alba) help it fly silently. Barn owls nest in barns and other buildings.

Feather care

Feathers take a constant battering and are regularly moulted and renewed, usually once a year. Even so, they need constant care and servicing. Careful combing with the beak links the hooks on the feather barbules together again like the teeth of a zip-fastener.

Most birds have a large oil gland near the base of the tail. The bird takes oil with its beak and coats its feathers individually to keep them supple and waterproof. Some, such as herons and parrots, produce a fine talc-like dust called powder-down, from special feathers.

Because flying uses a great deal of energy, birds tend to eat food that is full of calories. Some birds eat fish, some eat nuts, others eat nectar, or insect larvae, or sugar-laden fruit. Birds of prey can even eat small mammals. Birds have developed a wide variety of beaks which enable them to eat these different types of food.

The beak is a lightweight structure made of keratin. It is used only to gather and bite food; it cannot chew, though in some birds, parts of the beak have developed which are very similar to teeth.

Instead, birds break up their food in part of the gut called the gizzard. Because the gizzard lies in the middle of the body it cannot unbalance the bird while it is flying. Sometimes there are small stones in the gizzard which help to grind up the food so it can be digested.

Birds of the parrot family have strong hooked beaks for breaking open nuts and seeds. This blue and yellow macaw (Ara ararauna) lives in the wild in South America.

Birds' feet also vary tremendously in size and shape, depending on where and how they live. Most have three or four toes, though the ostrich has only two. Some birds – such as swifts and shearwaters – hardly ever land and can barely walk at all. At the other extreme, ostriches and kiwis cannot fly, and rely on their legs and feet to get around. Small birds move by hopping but larger birds, which are heavier, walk instead.

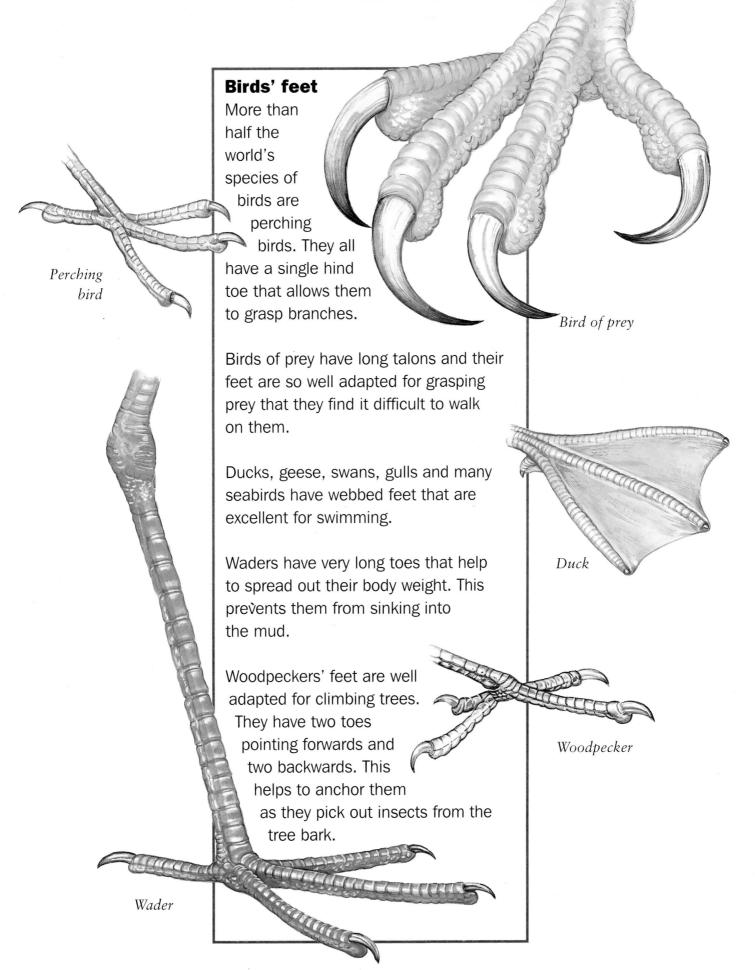

Birds' feet

More than half the world's species of birds are perching birds. They all have a single hind toe that allows them to grasp branches.

Birds of prey have long talons and their feet are so well adapted for grasping prey that they find it difficult to walk on them.

Ducks, geese, swans, gulls and many seabirds have webbed feet that are excellent for swimming.

Waders have very long toes that help to spread out their body weight. This prevents them from sinking into the mud.

Woodpeckers' feet are well adapted for climbing trees. They have two toes pointing forwards and two backwards. This helps to anchor them as they pick out insects from the tree bark.

Perching bird

Bird of prey

Duck

Woodpecker

Wader

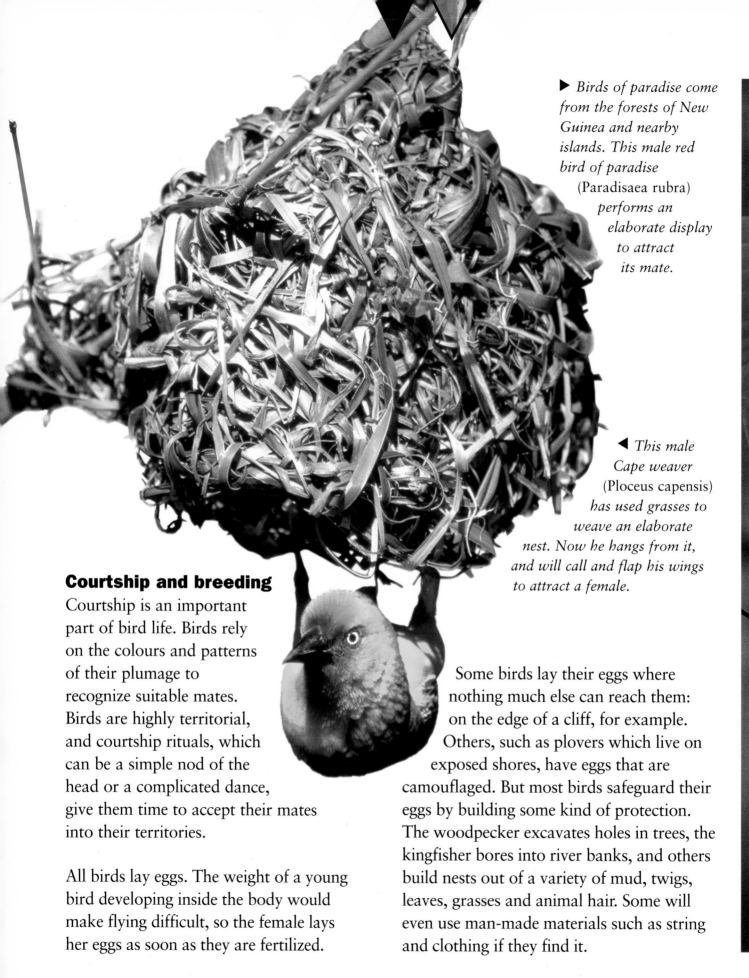

▶ *Birds of paradise come from the forests of New Guinea and nearby islands. This male red bird of paradise* (Paradisaea rubra) *performs an elaborate display to attract its mate.*

◀ *This male Cape weaver* (Ploceus capensis) *has used grasses to weave an elaborate nest. Now he hangs from it, and will call and flap his wings to attract a female.*

Courtship and breeding

Courtship is an important part of bird life. Birds rely on the colours and patterns of their plumage to recognize suitable mates. Birds are highly territorial, and courtship rituals, which can be a simple nod of the head or a complicated dance, give them time to accept their mates into their territories.

All birds lay eggs. The weight of a young bird developing inside the body would make flying difficult, so the female lays her eggs as soon as they are fertilized.

Some birds lay their eggs where nothing much else can reach them: on the edge of a cliff, for example. Others, such as plovers which live on exposed shores, have eggs that are camouflaged. But most birds safeguard their eggs by building some kind of protection. The woodpecker excavates holes in trees, the kingfisher bores into river banks, and others build nests out of a variety of mud, twigs, leaves, grasses and animal hair. Some will even use man-made materials such as string and clothing if they find it.

As a developing embryo is not able to keep itself warm enough, eggs need to be incubated. This is a very risky business as birds are particularly vulnerable to predators while they are sitting. A few birds avoid the hazardous duty altogether: the cuckoo lays its eggs in the nests of other birds, while the mallee fowl deposits its eggs in a large mound built by the male. The mound has vegetation at its core and is covered in sand. As the vegetation rots it produces heat which incubates the eggs.

Senses

Birds have very good eyesight and hearing. But their other senses, such as taste and smell, are very poorly developed.

Birds of prey have eyes that face forwards and give them binocular vision. This is important for judging distance, and vital for birds that swoop down from great heights to pick up small prey. Birds which are hunted themselves tend to have eyes on either side of the head. This allows them to see all around them, and is very helpful for spotting predators. Some owls can hunt in complete darkness, using their acute sense of hearing to detect the exact position of their prey.

Mammals

THE FIRST MAMMALS EVOLVED FROM REPTILES about 200 million years ago, at a time when dinosaurs dominated the land. These early mammals were probably small shrew-like creatures. It would have been another 100 million years or more, when the dinosaurs had died out, before mammals began to diversify and become the most dominant land vertebrates themselves. Mammals generally have hairy, smooth, dry skin and all have lungs to breathe air. They can regulate their body temperatures and they feed their young on milk.

Though it lays eggs, the duck-billed platypus (Ornithorhynchus anatinus) *is classified as a mammal because it is covered in hair and produces milk for its young.*

Characteristics of mammals:
▶ have hair on their bodies
▶ breathe with lungs
▶ can control their body temperature internally
▶ have internal fertilization
▶ feed their young on milk.

There are over 4,000 species of mammals, adapted to almost every way of life. Mammals have colonized oceans, rivers, land, mountains and deserts. They have become adapted in all sorts of ways to cope with their environments.

There are three main groups of mammals: monotremes, marsupials and placental mammals. These groups differ in the way they raise their young.

Monotremes

There are only two families of monotremes, the platypus and the spiny ant-eaters, also known as echidnas. Unlike other mammals, monotremes lay eggs. However, when the young have hatched they are not left to find food for themselves. Instead, the mother develops glands on her belly which produce milk.

Marsupials

Marsupial mammals were once widespread but now only 300 species remain, mostly in Australasia.

The marsupials do not lay eggs but they give birth to young that are not yet fully formed. These 'neonates', as they are called, complete their development in a pouch on the mother's abdomen.

▲ *Because the sea supports their bodies, whales have been able to grow larger than other mammals. This killer whale (Orcinus orca) is nursing her three-day-old calf, which may grow up to 9 m long.*

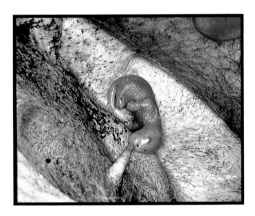

▲ *The kangaroo 'neonate' is blind, naked and only a few centimetres in length. When it is born it wades through the thick fur of its mother's abdomen to the pouch. Once there it fastens onto one of four teats and starts to feed. This is the newborn of a grey kangaroo (Macropus giganteus).*

Placental 'true' mammals

By far the majority of mammals are placental mammals. In this group, the young complete their development inside the mother's body, in the uterus. Here they receive all the nourishment they need from the mother's blood, via the placenta. Safe inside the mother's body, they are protected from the dangers of the external environment. Whales and seals, for example, can carry their unborn young even as they swim for months through freezing seas. The placenta is one of the reasons why mammals have had such success in colonizing the whole of the earth.

This giant anteater (Myrmecophaga tridactyla) of Brazil lives almost entirely on ants and termites. It has no teeth but a long tongue, and uses its claws to break into the nests of its prey.

Mammalian diets

Mammals have adapted in different ways, depending on what they eat. There are mammals, such as the hedgehog, which feed on insects. They are known as insectivores. Mammals such as sheep and horses, monkeys and giraffes eat only plant materials. They are the herbivores. Others, such as cats and dogs, eat other animals and are called carnivores. Animals that eat both plants and animals are known as omnivores.

Insectivores, herbivores and carnivores are groups which are described by their eating habits and are not part of a formal classification system. However, they are helpful descriptions when looking at the ways in which mammals have adapted.

Insectivores

Insectivores are commonly small, nocturnal mammals with long, narrow snouts, perfect for poking through leaf litter in search of insects. Their bodies are usually covered with short, dense fur, though in some, such as hedgehogs, some of the hairs have developed into spines.

Insectivores often have small ears and small eyes with poor vision. However, their senses of smell and hearing are usually sharp.

Some insectivores live on the ground, some burrow, others climb and a few spend part of their time in water. They feed on insects, grubs, snails and occasionally on helpless vertebrates such as young birds. Many are extremely active and constantly need to refuel with large quantities of food.

Many insectivores have a lot of teeth – up to forty. But those that eat ants and termites often have a long sticky tongue.

The pangolin has a most amazing tongue: the biggest has a tongue that can extend 40 cm from its mouth. It is so long that the sheath that houses it reaches right down the animal's chest, to its pelvis. The pangolin has no teeth at all. It collects ants and termites with the mucus on its tongue and swallows them whole. The meal is then mashed up by the stomach, which is horny and sometimes contains pebbles to help with the grinding process.

The majority of bats eat insects and may eat as many as 3,000 in one night. Bats like this serotine bat (Vespertilio serotinus) *find their prey by sending out high-pitched sounds that bounce back from objects, such as insects, in their path.*

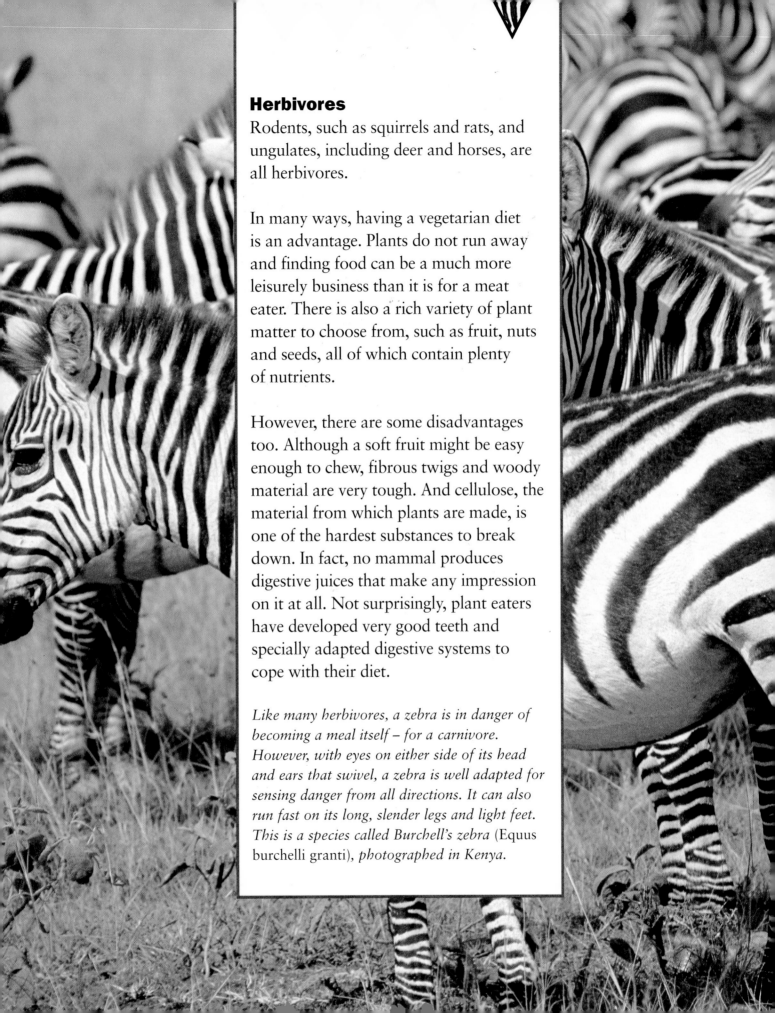

Herbivores

Rodents, such as squirrels and rats, and ungulates, including deer and horses, are all herbivores.

In many ways, having a vegetarian diet is an advantage. Plants do not run away and finding food can be a much more leisurely business than it is for a meat eater. There is also a rich variety of plant matter to choose from, such as fruit, nuts and seeds, all of which contain plenty of nutrients.

However, there are some disadvantages too. Although a soft fruit might be easy enough to chew, fibrous twigs and woody material are very tough. And cellulose, the material from which plants are made, is one of the hardest substances to break down. In fact, no mammal produces digestive juices that make any impression on it at all. Not surprisingly, plant eaters have developed very good teeth and specially adapted digestive systems to cope with their diet.

Like many herbivores, a zebra is in danger of becoming a meal itself – for a carnivore. However, with eyes on either side of its head and ears that swivel, a zebra is well adapted for sensing danger from all directions. It can also run fast on its long, slender legs and light feet. This is a species called Burchell's zebra (Equus burchelli granti), *photographed in Kenya.*

▼ *Mammals' teeth reflect the type of food they eat. A rodent has large incisors that it uses for gnawing woody vegetation. These incisors grow throughout the animal's life and are continuously being worn down and sharpened.*

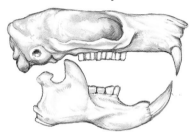

▼ *Herbivores such as the rhinoceros, which graze on grasses, do not have incisors at all. Their large flat molars and premolars are ideal for grinding up softer vegetation.*

▼ *Carnivores have large canine teeth to tear into flesh. Their molars and premolars have sharp edges that can cut meat.*

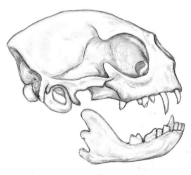

The common dormouse (Muscardinus avellanarius) *hibernates during winter. In cooler parts of the world, most plants disappear in winter, leaving herbivores with little or nothing to eat. Hibernation reduces the body's need for energy and, therefore, food.*

Although chewing begins to break down the plant cells, herbivores still have to find a way of digesting cellulose further. To do this they rely on help from bacteria. Certain bacteria produce an enzyme that dissolves cellulose, and herbivores have cultures of these in their stomachs. The bacteria make a meal of the cellulose and the animal can then absorb the cell contents. Even so, the digestion of a meal can take a long time and herbivores have evolved different ways of dealing with this problem.

Cows and sheep regurgitate their food. Once swallowed, the food passes into the rumen, a chamber of the stomach that contains a large number of bacteria. There it is churned back and forth for several hours until eventually the pulp is brought up a mouthful at a time to be chewed – a process often called 'chewing the cud'. Eventually, the mouthful is swallowed again. This time it goes straight to the stomach proper, from where it is absorbed.

Rabbits deal with the problem differently: they eat their food twice. After eating a meal for the first time, they pass soft pellets in their burrows, which they then eat. Only after the second time do the rabbits deposit dry pellets outside their burrows.

Elephants have stomachs big enough to provide a long period of digestion. An elephant's meal takes about two and a half days to pass through its body.

Carnivores

Carnivores include the cat and the dog families. Hunting is a more complicated activity than grazing, and these mammals have larger brains than their herbivorous cousins. Their senses are highly developed – they have acute hearing and eyesight – and because their eyes face forward they can judge distances, an essential skill when deciding on the right moment to pounce. Many can also see in the dark and have a fine sense of smell that they use both for trailing prey and communicating with each other.

The ability to move quickly is a definite advantage for a hunter, and cats' bodies are particularly well suited for running at speed. Most have powerful, muscular legs, although the cheetah, which is the fastest of all the cats, has long thin legs. Its flexible spine allows it to stretch out fully when running and reach speeds of 110 kph, although only for a few hundred metres.

Two lions (Panthera leo), *a male and a female, watch a herd of topi* (Damaliscus korrigum) *in Kenya.*

Lions are slower – their top speed is around 80 kph – and they rely on stealth, creeping close to their prey by moving slowly. Unlike most cats, lions will also hunt in teams.

The cats are the most efficient killers. They keep their claws sharp by pulling them back into sheaths when they are not being used. When they attack, they hook their victim with their claws and bite its neck, severing the spinal cord and bringing a swift death.

The slim legs and light feet of the dog family enable them to run long distances but they cannot run as fast as the cats. Hyenas only manage speeds of around 50 kph. They make up for their lack of pace by cunning. Usually hunting at night, and in packs, they will often test the herd to see which individuals are the weakest. Then, having selected a victim, they chase it, snapping at its heels until it is exhausted.

Although dogs and cats have strong skulls with powerful jaw muscles, they cannot chew: their jaws can only open and shut and cannot move from side to side. However, since meat is easier to digest than plants, this is not a problem. These mammals also have long, dagger-like canine teeth that they use for stabbing and holding their prey and for slashing open its hide. They use their back teeth for shearing bones. It takes a pack of hyenas only about 15 minutes to devour a complete carcass, bones included.

Spotted hyenas (Crocuta crocuta) *eating freshly killed wildebeeste* (Connochaetes taurinus).

Animals
in water environments

WATERY ENVIRONMENTS offer abundant opportunities for life. Fish are ideally adapted to thrive in water, but they are not the only vertebrates who live there: there are members of all the vertebrate classes that spend some or all of their time in water.

An otter's fur is very dense, which makes it an effective insulator in water. It has an inner downy layer that traps warm air next to the body, and an outer waterproof layer.

Known as the edible frog (Rana esculenta), *this species remains virtually hidden from predators as it swims with just its eyes above the surface.*

Like fish, the tadpoles of frogs and toads have gills as well as powerful tails and fins which enable them to spend this stage of their life cycle completely in water. As adults, most still return to water, particularly to breed, and their muscular back legs and webbed feet help them swim. Like many other animals that spend only part of their time in water, such as otters and crocodiles, frogs can swim with just their eyes, ears and nostrils above the surface. This helps them to avoid predators or to approach prey.

Whales and dolphins spend all their lives in water, but like other mammals, they breathe air. To do this they must make regular visits to the surface. However, whales breathe much more efficiently than other mammals. Whereas we humans breathe out only about 15 per cent of the air in our lungs, a whale can empty its lungs of about 90 per cent of the air. A whale also has a very high concentration of a substance called myoglobin in its muscles. Myoglobin stores oxygen. So the fin-back whale, for example, can dive to a depth of 500 m and swim for 40 minutes before it needs to surface for air. As a whale's nostrils are positioned on top of its head it can breathe with its eyes and ears still below the surface. This is an advantage, as it allows the animal to continue to be aware of changes in its environment.

The dipper (Cinclus mexicanus) *is a bird that lives near mountain streams. It can swim, dive or even walk along the bottom of the river bed. It uses its wings to swim to the bottom. Once there, the pressure of the water on its wings and tail keeps it down while it searches for food.*

Animals
of the air

Flying squirrels have flaps of skin down the sides of their bodies that act as parachutes. The flattened tail serves as a rudder and a brake. This is the southern flying squirrel, (Glaucomys volans).

THERE ARE TWO WAYS OF TRAVELLING THROUGH AIR: gliding and flying. Animals that fly have wings which they use to propel themselves forwards and upwards, using their own power against gravity. These animals can also use their wings for gliding. Gliders, on the other hand, cannot gain height and are only able to slow down the rate at which they fall. Most have folds of loose skin which they can spread out to increase their surface area against the air. As with animals that live in water, animals that move quickly through the air are streamlined.

Animals that fly

Of the vertebrates, only birds and bats are capable of flying. Birds can fly because of the special shape of their wings: they have a rounded leading edge, are flattened underneath and curved on top. This aerofoil shape produces lift in the same way that an aircraft wing does.

Bats' wings consist of skin stretched over the forelimb and down to the hindlimb and tail. Like birds, their bodies are relatively light. The bones of their limbs are hollow and their other bones are slight. Their arm muscles are much more powerful for their size than those of other mammals. Being able to fly enables insect-eating birds and bats to catch their prey on the wing and this gives them an advantage over animals that cannot get off the ground.

Animals that glide

A number of animals that glide are tree dwellers. A few tree-living frogs can travel 15 m or so through the air, about a hundred times their body length, by gliding. The web of skin between their toes is greatly enlarged so that each foot acts like a small parachute. When the frog leaps off the branch of a tree it glides gently downwards, usually to another tree.

The colugo is a mammal about the size of a large rabbit. Its entire body – from its neck to the end of its tail – is covered by a cloak of furry skin. When it stretches out its legs the cloak becomes a gliding membrane and the animal is able to glide from tree to tree.

A flying fish gets up speed in the water, breaks through the surface, and can then glide for hundreds of metres by spreading out its unusually broad pectoral fins.

Land Animals

WITH THE EXCEPTION OF SNAKES AND LEGLESS LIZARDS, vertebrate animals that live on land support their body weight on limbs with strong bones.

A young white-fronted capuchin monkey (Cabus albifrons) of the Amazon rain forest in Brazil, using its tail as well as its legs to climb a tree.

Most land vertebrates have four legs and are known as tetrapods. When a tetrapod is standing still it is perfectly balanced on its four legs, rather like a table. However, as soon as it lifts one leg to move, it has to shift its centre of gravity so that it does not topple over. Walking involves constantly shifting weight diagonally forwards and backwards to maintain balance. Some animals, such as rabbits, have their centre of gravity towards the back of their bodies. This means they can lift both their front legs at the same time and sit on their haunches. From this position they are able to look around with ease. A kangaroo has a centre of gravity so far back that the animal is only prevented from falling backwards by its muscular tail.

Adaptation for movement

Animals that burrow underground have relatively streamlined bodies. Burrowing mammals, such as moles, generally have one pair of feet that are spade-like and which they use for digging. Some also burrow through the earth with the aid of huge front teeth. Their fur is normally very short and thick and does not have any particular direction of growth which means that it does not drag against the soil.

Jumping is a very good way to cover ground quickly. Animals that jump have long, muscular hind legs. Many also have a tail which helps them balance. Some jumpers, such as the kangaroo, use their rear limbs for both leaping and landing. Others, such as frogs, land on their front limbs first.

Animals that live in trees are well adapted for climbing. They all have some means of being able to hold on to branches and many are also light in weight, which makes the task of climbing easier. Those which are very small and light, such as squirrels and some lizards, can run along branches by gripping the bark with their claws. Others, such as tree-climbing frogs and geckos, have feet which can stick to the surface of even the smoothest branches. Heavier animals, such as lemurs, monkeys and apes, grip branches by clasping their fingers and toes around them.

Many tree-dwelling animals have tails that help them balance and may also be used for clinging onto branches.

The mole (Talpa europaea) *cannot see and uses its sensitive nose to detect its prey.*

Animal adaptations to climate

ALL ANIMALS NEED to be able to regulate their body temperature. They also all need sufficient water. This can be difficult in the desert – where temperatures change dramatically in the course of a day and water is in short supply – and in the polar regions, where temperatures are below freezing all year round. Animals have become adapted to cope with these different climates in a variety of ways.

Camels can go for long periods without drinking. However, when water is available they may drink litres at a time.

Desert dwellers

Many desert animals are light in colour and this reflects sunlight away from their bodies. Reptiles, such as lizards, move in and out of the sun during the day to keep warm without overheating. At night, some huddle together in rock crevices to keep warm, or burrow into the ground. The kangaroo rat has large ears that lose heat and help keep the animal cool during the day. At night it burrows to keep warm.

Desert-living animals have to be able to survive shortages of water. Some never drink at all, making do with the fluids in the plants and animals they eat. Many are also able to prevent themselves from losing much water. The kangaroo rat, for example, excretes only very concentrated urine.

Food may be in short supply in the desert, too. The gila monster is a large poisonous lizard that stores fat in its thick tail. It can live on this fat for months when food is scarce. Camels also store food, in their humps. In periods of starvation the hump gets smaller as the animal uses up its store.

Surviving the cold

Birds and mammals that live in the polar regions are very well insulated. Seals and whales have a thick layer of blubber under their skin which keeps them warm. The polar bear combines a thick layer of fat with a dense fur coat. The bear's white fur reflects heat back to its body. Its hairs are hollow: ultraviolet light from the sun can pass through the hairs to be absorbed by the black skin underneath.

Small mammals, such as lemmings, excavate a system of tunnels and chambers where they remain active during the winter. However, the Arctic ground squirrel hibernates, its body temperature falling to below 0 °C.

Birds are better adapted to survive extreme cold than mammals as their downy feathers are a much better insulator than hair. However, many birds migrate to warmer regions so that they avoid very cold winters.

Emperor penguins (Aptenodytes forsteri) *are so well-insulated they can survive on the Antarctic ice-cap even in winter.*

The future for animals

NEW SPECIES ARE BEING DISCOVERED all the time as biologists continue to explore every corner of the earth. However, species are also disappearing. As we humans continue to clear enormous tracts of land to grow crops and build cities, we are destroying the habitats in which many species live. Although animals do adapt to new environments, this is a process that can take millions of years. People are causing changes on a daily basis: far too fast for living things to adjust to successfully.

We are destroying species in other ways, too. Many animals are hunted for small parts of their bodies, even though they are now nearly extinct. For example, the rhino is still being hunted for its horn and elephants for their tusks. Other animals have been hunted for their skin: crocodile and snake skins are used to make leather shoes and bags, while the skins of leopards and seals are made into fur coats.

Our farms and industries use and produce harmful chemicals that pollute the air, the land and the oceans and have made it impossible for some species to survive. Accidents, such as oil spills, have also killed large numbers of animals.

This female black rhino (Rhinoceros bicornis) *has been killed for its horn.*

The problem is vast. According to the International Union for the Conservation of Nature (IUCN), 25 per cent of all mammal species (including 46 per cent of primates, 36 per cent of insectivores, and 33 per cent of pigs and antelopes) and 11 per cent of all bird species are threatened with extinction.

To ensure the survival of endangered species we need to understand their needs and monitor their populations. These biologists are fixing a radio collar to a tiger (Panthera tigris) so that they can track its movements.

Modern farming methods include selective breeding, in which animals are bred for particular characteristics. Cattle may be bred for increased meat or milk yield, sheep for better quality wool, and hens for improved egg production. This process forces species to change in specific ways very quickly. But rather than adapting for their own survival, selective breeding encourages features which suit human needs.

More recently, scientists have started to use a technique called genetic engineering. This process involves changing the genetic material of a living organism, sometimes by introducing genes from another species, in order to change its characteristics. Genetic engineering has the potential to cure diseases, but it may also cause serious problems, perhaps by breeding types of bacteria or virus that are harmful.

It is clear that the responsibility for caring for the animal kingdom lies with one particular mammal: human beings. But this requires us to take the interests of the animal kingdom as seriously as we take our own.

Chimpanzees (Pan troglodytes) are highly intelligent African apes. Studies of chimpanzee and human chromosomes suggest that they share 99 per cent of the same genes.

Glossary

Bacteria Tiny, single-celled living things. Some bacteria can cause disease.

Binocular vision A type of vision that uses two eyes facing forwards to produce a 3-dimensional image.

Brackish Describes water that is slightly salty. Brackish water is found in estuaries where rivers flow into the sea and fresh water and salt water mix.

Camouflage Colours or structures that allow an animal to blend with its surroundings and avoid being seen by other animals.

Cartilage A tissue found in some animal skeletons. Cartilage is softer and more flexible than bone.

Cellulose Tough, fibrous material found in plant cell walls.

Colonize When a species spreads into a new habitat.

Diversify To become modified (into different varieties) in order to adapt to different environments.

Embryo The early developmental stage of a living thing. The embryo forms after fertilization.

Enzymes Substances that can speed up the rates of chemical reactions in living things.

Evolve To develop gradually by natural processes, usually as a result of many small changes over a long period of time.

Excrete To get rid of harmful or unwanted waste matter from the body.

Fertilization The process that occurs in sexual reproduction when two sex cells, a female egg and a male sperm, become joined. 'Internal fertilization' takes place inside the body, normally of the female. Fertilization that takes place outside the body is called 'external fertilization'.

Genes/genetic Genes are found in cells of organisms. They carry information about the characteristics of a living thing and are passed on to offspring during reproduction.

Genus A group of species that have many characteristics in common.

Gills Organs that fish and many other aquatic animals use for respiration. Oxygen from the water passes across the gills and into the bloodstream.

Hibernate To spend the cold winter in a deep sleep.

Incubate To keep eggs warm so that the embryos can develop and hatch.

Larva (plural larvae) A stage between hatching and becoming an adult in those species where the young have a very different appearance and way of life from the adult. Examples include tadpoles (of frogs and toads) and caterpillars (of butterflies and moths).

Metamorphosis The period during which an animal changes from a larva to an adult. For example, a tadpole goes through metamorphosis to become an adult frog.

Mucus A slimy substance that lubricates and protects parts of the body.

Nectar A sugary liquid produced by some flowers.

Nocturnal Describes animals that are active at night.

Organisms Living things.

Osmosis The movement of a water through a semi-permeable membrane (a membrane that only allows some substances to pass through it) from a dilute solution to a more concentrated solution.

Placenta An organ that develops in the uterus of most pregnant mammals. The placenta nourishes and maintains the developing embryo. It is attached to the embryo by the umbilical cord.

Predator An animal that hunts or kills other animals for food.

Prey An animal that is hunted, killed and eaten by another animal.

Primate A type of mammal that includes human beings, apes, monkeys, lemurs and bushbabies. Primates have hands and feet that are adapted for grasping and climbing. They also have relatively large brains.

Respire To take in oxygen and give out carbon dioxide. Animals that live on land respire by breathing air in and out of their lungs. Respiration leads to the release of energy from food.

Rodents A group of mammals that includes rats, squirrels and beavers. All rodents have large pairs of incisor (front) teeth that continue to grow throughout life and are used for biting and gnawing.

Species A group of animals that all have the same basic physical appearance and which can reproduce successfully with each other.

Streamlined Having a smooth shape that can easily move through air or water.

Territorial Describes an animal that defends the particular area in which it lives from other members of the same species.

Tropics The area between the tropics of Cancer and Capricorn, which are approximately $23\frac{1}{2}°$ north and south of the Equator. This region is hot all year, with an average temperature of 20 °C.

Ungulates A group of mammals that has hooves.

Uterus The organ in female mammals in which offspring develop before birth.

Further information

Books

Animals by Habitat series (Wayland, 1996)

Dangerous Animals by Dr Susan Lumpkin (Macdonald Young Books, 1995)

The Marshall Illustrated Encyclopedia of Animals (Marshall Editions, 1998)

Natural World series: 12 books on individual animals in the wild (Wayland, 1999–2000)

Nature Encyclopedia (Dorling Kindersley, 1998)

Reptiles by Carson Creagh (Macdonald Young Books, 1996)

What is a ... Mammal / Bird / Amphibian / Reptile by Robert Snedden (Belitha, 1993–94)

Posters

Classifying Animals (Chart and Notes) by Roger Hore (PCET, 1997)

CD-ROMs

Exploring Land Habitats (Wayland, 1997)
Exploring Water Habitats (Wayland, 1997)

Useful addresses and web sites

The Natural History Museum
Cromwell Road, London SW7 5BD
www.nhm.ac.uk/education

World Wide Fund for Nature UK
Panda House, Weyside Park
Godalming, Surrey GU7 1XR
www.wwf-uk.org

Care for the Wild International
1 Ashfolds, Horsham Road
Rusper, West Sussex RH12 4QX
www.careforthewild.org.uk

Royal Society for the Protection of Birds
The Lodge, Sandy
Bedfordshire SG19 2DL
www.rspb.org.uk

The Mammal Society
15 Cloisters Business Centre
8 Battersea Park Road
London SW8 4BG
www.abdn.ac.uk/mammal/

Reptile Protection Trust
College Gates
2 Deansway, Worcester WR1 2JD

Picture acknowledgements

Cover: Bruce Coleman: leopard (Christer Fredriksson), owl (Joe McDonald), fish (Pacific Stock), frog (Rod Williams). Tony Stone: toucan (Stuart Westmoreland), iguana (Werner H Muller).
Inside: Bruce Coleman 6 (Franco Banfi), 6–7 (Andrew J Purcell), 8 (Hans Reinhard), 9 (Kim Taylor), 11 (Mark Carwardine), 14–15 (Jane Burton), 15 (Jane Burton), 16 (M P L Fogden), 17 (John Cancalosi), 19 (Gerald Cubitt), 21 (Fred Bruemmer), 22 (Bruce Coleman Inc), 23 (Kim Taylor), 24 (Jane Burton), 26 (HPH Photography), 27 (Brian J Coates), 28 (Francisco Futil), 29 top (Ken Balcomb), 30 (Luiz Claudio Marigo), 31 (Kim Taylor), 32 (Luiz Claudio Marigo), 33 (George McCarthy), 35 (Peter Davey), 36 top (Paul Van Gaalen), 36 bottom (Ingo Arndt), 37 (Dieter & Mary Plage), 38 (Kim Taylor), 40 (Luiz Claudio Marigo), 41 (Andrew Purcell), 43 (Hans Reinhard), 44 (Peter Davey), 45 top (Michael P Price). Natural History Photo Library 12 (Daniel Heuclin), 34 (Martin Harvey), 39 (Norbert Wu). Oxford Scientific Films 4–5 (Martyn Colbeck), 29 bottom (Alan Root/Okapia). Tony Stone *title page* (Art Wolfe), 20 (Ron Dahlquist), 45 bottom (Tim Davis). Wayland Picture Library 2, 42.
Artwork: pages 5 and 23 by Simon Borrough; pages 10, 13, 18 and 25 by Peter Bull Art Studio.

Index